Afternoon Tea: Downton Abbey Style Afternoon Tea

Inspiration and How to Host the Perfect Afternoon Tea Party at Your Home

Table of Contents

Thank you! _____ 2

Introduction _____ 5

Chapter 1 – The History behind the English Afternoon Tea _ 6

Chapter 2 – Choosing the Right Tea for Your Service _____ 8

Chapter 3 – Recipes that Go Well with Afternoon Tea _____ 12

Chapter 4 – Afternoon Tea Essentials _____ 28

Chapter 5 – Proper Etiquette _____ 32

Conclusion _____ 37

Check Out My Other Books! _____ 38

Greetings from the Lean Stone Publishing Company _____ 41

Thank you!

Thank you for buying this book!

If you enjoy the book and get some value from it, I would appreciate if you could **leave an honest review** on the Amazon store after finishing.

Thank you and enjoy the book!

***

Receive updates on new book releases, book promotions and much more from Tadio Diller by signing up to the e-mail list: **http://bit.ly/list_tadiodiller_cs**

***

Follow us, Lean Stone Publishing, the publishing company that published this book. You will receive information on upcoming book launches, free book promotions and much more. Sign up to this e-mail list: **http://bit.ly/list_lsp_cs**

***

Like us at **www.facebook.com/leanstonepublishing**

Follow us on Twitter **@leanstonebooks**

The trademarks that are used are without any consent, and the publication of the trademark is without permission or backing by the trademark owner. All trademarks and brands within this book are for clarifying purposes only and are the owned by the owners themselves, not affiliated with this document.

Introduction

I want to thank you and congratulate you for buying the book, *"Afternoon Tea: Downton Abbey Style Afternoon Tea - Inspiration and How to Host the Perfect Afternoon Tea Party at Your Home."*

This book contains proven steps and strategies for conducting a "proper" afternoon tea service just like they do on *Downton Abbey*.

In this day and age wherein most people's idea of entertainment is watching a couple of drug cooks escaping from gangsters or, if you prefer, a group of misfits running away from zombies, a show that breaks the mold like *Downton Abbey* is a breath of fresh air.

Downton Abbey tells the story of an aristocratic family living in the post-Edwardian era, which is around the time the Titanic sank. Besides being a darned good dramatic series (it has already won a couple of awards), *Downton Abbey* actually got people interested in the aristocratic lifestyle, more specifically in the way they conduct their afternoon tea service.

Americans are not really avid tea drinkers, not since the Boston Tea Party, so the idea of an afternoon tea service is completely alien for most folks. *Downton Abbey* is where most of them learned about it, and quite a lot of people actually want to make it a regular habit.

In this book, you will learn almost everything you need to know about hosting a prim and proper afternoon tea service, from choosing the tea, the china, and how to compose yourself properly in front of company. Hopefully, after reading this, you will be able to throw a tea service the likes of which will impress even the Dowager Countess of Grantham.

Thanks again for buying this book. I hope you enjoy it!

Chapter 1 – The History behind the English Afternoon Tea

"At half past three, the world stops for tea…" Or at least it used to. These days, even the English are too busy to have a proper afternoon tea party. This is quite unfortunate because afternoon tea was supposed to prevent lethargy, making people work more efficiently. Yes, even though afternoon tea is a pretty laid-back affair, it was first done because a noblewoman felt too tired in the middle of the afternoon.

The year was 1840 and, at the time, people were used to having only two meals every day: breakfast in the morning and dinner at around eight in the evening. Anna, the 7th Duchess of Bedford, complained to her staff that she always had a "sinking feeling" during the mid-afternoon, which was quite natural since she had not had a bite to eat since breakfast.

The solution the duchess came up with was for her attendants to bring a pot of hot tea and some small pastries and cakes up to her boudoir every afternoon so she could relax and recharge her energy. After some time, the Duchess of Bedford started inviting a couple of her friends over for afternoon tea and a walk around her garden.

Her afternoon habit became so popular that other high society women began having their own tea parties. Some of them, for the sake of decency, took their tea in their drawing rooms instead of the boudoir. From then on, once it hit mid-afternoon, people would draw their kettles, prepare tiny sandwiches, and chat with their dear friends and family.

Low Tea and High Tea

Now, this may come as a surprise to the uninitiated such as yourself, but in jolly old England, there are such things as low and high tea. You may think that the fancy afternoon tea is in fact the one synonymous with high tea (high society, the "high" life), but you would be wrong.

The terms high and low tea does not connote the host's social standing. It is actually descriptive of the way the tea is served. High tea means that it is served on the "high" dinner table and is typically served during the early evening, is around 6 or 7 PM.

High tea, besides the actual beverage, includes heartier fare like meats, poultry, and fish along with bread and certain cakes. It is also usually a replacement for afternoon tea and dinner; hence, the more substantial fare.

On the other hand, low tea, also known as afternoon tea, is served on a "low" table setting, like coffee tables, and is served with lighter snacks like sandwiches and teacakes.

Chapter 2 – Choosing the Right Tea for Your Service

Most people consider afternoon tea an actual meal, which is why you need to put in a bit of effort to serve your guests the best foods possible. This chapter will discuss the kinds of foods you need to include in your afternoon tea menu.

Tea is perhaps one of the most popular beverages in the world, which is why there are more than a thousand types of tea available today. There are no set rules as to the kind of tea you need to serve your guests. You can choose teas that have a strong robust taste, or you can serve something mild and delicate. It is all up to your personal preferences.

However, since this may be your first time to host a proper afternoon tea, and if you are like most North Americans who haven't the slightest idea about tea, then here are some of the most popular types along with their ideal steeping times.

Earl Grey Tea

This tea got its name from the second Earl Grey, the Prime Minister of England during the 1830's. Stories state that the PM received a gift of tea infused with bergamot (a type of orange) essential oil from a foreign diplomat. The bergamot gives the Earl Grey tea a slight citrusy flavor that supposedly mimics the flavor of the expensive Chinese teas. Today, Earl Grey can stand by itself as a proper type of tea.

Ideal Steeping Time - Between 3 to 5 minutes

Assam Tea

Named after the region in India where it comes from, Assam tea is a type of black tea popular for its brisk, malty flavor, and bright color. Although considered by many as a breakfast tea (which is why it is sometimes called English breakfast), Assam tea also works great for afternoon tea because it can give you that much-needed pick-me-up to help you get through the rest of the day.

Ideal Steeping Time - If you will be serving this tea with milk, you need to steep it for at least 7 minutes to extract a stronger flavor from the leaves. However, if you will be serving this tea straight up, 3 to 5 minutes of steeping will be enough.

Ceylon Tea

This tea comes from the island nation of Sri Lanka (formerly Ceylon), which actually made tea famous worldwide. Even though tea originally came from China, Ceylon, with its ideal soil composition and climate, allowed the country to produce high quality teas. There are actually different types of Ceylon tea (green, white, and black), but the one commonly used for afternoon tea is Ceylon black tea. This type can be quite expensive because each tealeaf is picked by hand to ensure quality.

Ideal Steeping Time: If you do not want your tea too strong, 3 minutes steeping time is fine. For a stronger blend, steep the loose leaf to no more than 5 minutes.

Gunpowder Green Tea

Typically, green tea does not have enough of a robust flavor to go well with the other fares included in afternoon tea, but Gunpowder green tea is an exception. Unlike other green teas that have a delicate and light flavor, Gunpowder tea has a rather "masculine" flavor profile, full bodied, and a hint of smokiness. This green tea originally came from the Zhejiang province in China, where they roll each individual leaf into small black pellets, making them vaguely resemble early gunpowder; hence, the name.

Rolling the leaves supposedly makes them more resistant to damage and allows them to retain most of their flavor by inhibiting oxidation. The rule of thumb when choosing Gunpowder green tea is that the bigger and shinier the pellets are, the better quality the tea is.

Ideal Steeping Time: 2 minutes or until all the tea pellets completely unfurl themselves and release all of their concentrated flavors.

Lapsang Souchong

Roughly translated, Lapsang Souchong means "sub-variety coming from Lapu Mountain." Unlike most other teas, traditional Lapsang Souchong tea is smoke-dried, specifically using pinewood as fuel. This gives this tea a distinct, smoky flavor that you will not find in any other varieties. The original Lapsang Souchong sourced from the Wuyi Mountains in China is one of the most expensive teas in the world, mainly because the growing area is small and the demand for the elegant beverage is continuously increasing.

The smoky and slightly citrusy flavor (thanks to the infusion of dried longan) of Lapsang Souchong goes well with the typical fare that accompanies afternoon tea.

Ideal Steeping Time: You need to be a bit more careful when brewing Lapsang Souchong because it tends to become bitter if you let it steep too long. To start, let the leaves steep for around two and a half minutes, and gradually adjust the time until you reach the optimal flavor to your liking.

Darjeeling Tea

Hailing from West Bengal in India, this black tea (which is technically oolong tea since it is not completely oxidized) has a fruity (reminiscent of French grapes) and somewhat floral taste, which is why it also goes by the moniker "Darjeeling champagne." The thing with Darjeeling tea is that even if it comes from the same plantation, its taste can vary depending on the time of year it was harvested.

Ideal Steeping Time: This is where it gets a bit tricky. Since the flavor of Darjeeling is not as uniform as that of the other types of teas, you need to do a bit of trial and error to get the taste just right. It is also recommended that you place the tealeaves directly at the bottom of the teapot and strain the liquid into another pot. Using the traditional metal tea ball is not recommended because the leaves will block the holes; thus, preventing a proper infusion.

These are only some popular tea varieties out there and, if you want, you can even blend different teas so you can achieve your own unique taste. However, it is recommended that you get the help of a professional brew master to ensure that your combination is actually palatable.

As mentioned earlier, there are no set rules as to the kind of tea you should serve in your afternoon tea service. It will all depend on you and your preferences.

Chapter 3 – Recipes that Go Well with Afternoon Tea

Although the star of the afternoon tea is, of course, the tea itself, you also need to serve items that are a bit more nourishing to complete the affair. A proper afternoon tea party should at least have a selection of different pastries, sandwiches and, if you were to give yourself a bit of time to prepare, some miniature cakes for your guests. Not only should these additional fares be tasty, they must also be aesthetically pleasing.

Since this is your first time hosting a "proper" afternoon tea, you may not have any idea what to serve your guests. To help ensure that your first foray to the high-class world is a success, here are some suggestions that you may want to include in your menu.

Sandwiches

Sandwiches are the easiest entrees that you can serve to your guests. You mostly only need to prepare their filling beforehand and assemble the sandwiches right after your guests start to arrive so they won't get too soggy. Here are a couple of simple (and some not-so-simple) sandwich recipes that you might want to try.

Smoked Salmon and Avocado on Rye

Ingredients:

1 large avocado

Chili paste (to taste)

The juice of 1 lime or half a lemon

Salt and pepper (to taste)

Rye bread

Mash the flesh of the avocado and mix in the chili paste (Tabasco sauce will suffice if you can't find chili paste), the juice of one lime (or half a lemon), and salt and pepper to taste. Spread the mixture over a slice of wholegrain rye bread and top it off with a couple of strips of thinly sliced smoked salmon and a lime wedge on the side.

You can also substitute roast turkey or chicken slices for the smoked salmon if you want to mix things up a bit.

Mini Salt Beef Bagels

Ingredients:

6 slices of salt beef (you can also use pastrami or roast beef if you wish)

3 mini bagels, sliced in two

100g crème fraiche (or sour cream)

A tablespoon of mustard

4 radishes, sliced really thin

2 tablespoons vinegar (white wine vinegar preferably)

1 teaspoon brown sugar

A handful of fresh watercress

In a bowl, mix the vinegar and sugar until combined thoroughly. Throw in the radish slices and allow them to pickle in the vinegar and sugar mixture for at least 30 minutes. It is actually best to make this the night before your afternoon tea. Right before your guests start to arrive, combine the crème fraiche and mustard and spread the mixture on top of the bagel slices. Top the bagels with a slice of the salt beef, a couple of slices of pickled radish and a couple of sprigs of watercress. Sprinkle a bit of freshly ground black pepper on top and serve immediately.

Creamy Egg and Watercress Sandwiches

Ingredients:

6 small dinner rolls

2 medium, organic eggs, hard-boiled

1 spring onion, chopped coarsely

2 tablespoons crème fraiche or sour cream

Enough watercress for 6 small sandwiches

Peel the eggs and mash them together with the spring onions and crème fraiche. Season with salt and pepper to taste. Split the rolls in half and spread the egg and crème fraiche mixture on the bottom half of each roll. Top with a couple of sprigs of watercress before placing the top half of the roll.

Scones

Scones are the quintessential snack item associated with tea. Some Englishmen cannot even think of having tea without a plate of scones and their favorite jam on the side. Admittedly, you will need to allot enough time to make scones, but the beauty of them is that you can make them the night before, freeze them and reheat them in the oven before your guests come.

Classic Scones Recipe

Ingredients:

A cup and a half of self-raising flour, add in a bit more for dusting the tops of the scones.

A pinch of salt

1 teaspoon baking powder

2/3 of a stick of butter, cubed

3 tablespoons brown sugar

1 teaspoon of vanilla extract

The juice of 1 lemon

¾ a cup of milk

1 egg, beaten lightly

Preheat your oven to 220 degrees C. In a large mixing bowl, sift together the flour and baking powder. Using your hands, combine the flour and butter until you get the consistency of fine breadcrumbs. Mix in the sugar afterwards.

Place the milk in a microwave-safe bowl and heat the milk until it is warm, but not scalding hot. Take the milk out of the microwave oven and add the lemon juice and vanilla extract.

Make a well in the center of the dry ingredients and then pour in your warm milk mixture. Combine the ingredients thoroughly using a rubber spatula. Do not worry if the dough may seem a bit too wet right now.

Place an empty baking tray in the oven and let it heat up considerably. Dust your work area (you can use a large cutting board) with a bit of flour to prevent the dough from sticking. Place your dough onto your work surface. Using your hands and a bit more flour, massage the dough until it is a bit firmer than before. Fold the dough 2 to 3 times to make the outside skin smoother. Flatten out your dough until it is roughly half an inch thick.

Using a two-inch cookie cutter, punch about four scones out of the flattened dough. Rework the dough and cut out a couple more scones. You can make around 7 to 8 scones out of this recipe.

Take the baking tray from the oven and carefully place the scones on the surface. Brush the tops of the scones with the beaten egg before returning the tray in the oven. Bake the scones for around 10 minutes or until they have risen a bit and the tops are golden brown.

Serve the scones while still warm with some clotted cream or your favorite jam.

Apple Scones with Blueberry Compote

This is a fancier version of the classic scones. The apples and blueberries will work quite well with a citrusy tea like Darjeeling. This may take a bit more work, but it will surely impress your guests.

Ingredients:

1 cup self-raising flour

Half a stick of butter

4 tablespoons brown sugar

¼ teaspoon ground cinnamon

½ cup of milk, plus a bit more for brushing the tops of the scones

1 large apple, diced

Preheat your oven to 220 degrees Celsius. Pour your flour into a large mixing bowl. Using your fingers, mash the butter into the flour until it reaches the consistency of wet sand. At this point, mix in the sugar, cinnamon, and diced apple.

Create a well in the middle of the flour mixture and pour the milk into it. Mix everything until the dough starts to take shape on its own. Tip the contents of the bowl onto a cutting board lightly dusted with flour. Massage the dough a bit and then pat into a circle that is around an inch and a half thick.

Using a 2-inch dough cutter, punch out your scones. Make sure to use every last bit of the dough. This recipe should allow you to make around 6 to 7 decently sized scones. Arrange your scones on a baking sheet lightly dusted with some flour. Brush their tops with some milk and place in the pre-heated oven and bake for 15 to 20 minutes, or until the scones have risen and the tops are golden brown.

Allow the scones to cool for a bit on the tray. To serve, split the scones in two, spread a dollop of clotted cream and a bit of blueberry compote in the middle and plop the top back on.

Teacakes and Buns

The sandwiches and scones are quite simple to make so you can get the hang of making them after just one try. Teacakes and buns, on the other hand, will take a bit more finesse and attention to detail. The following recipes, though not overly complicated, might be quite difficult for those who have no prior experience in baking. You may want to practice a bit more on making scones before you try your hand at making the following pastries.

Hot Cross Buns

This is a classic English teatime food. These spiced buns will fill your home with a nice, welcoming smell and make your guests wish out loud that you would invite them back again for afternoon tea.

Ingredients:

2 cups of white flour

2 7g packets of quick raising yeast

¼ cup of sugar

2/3 cup of warm milk

1 organic egg, lightly beaten

Half a stick of unsalted butter, melted

Some vegetable oil for greasing the baking pan

1 teaspoon cinnamon, ground

½ teaspoon allspice

A pinch of grated nutmeg

½ cup dried currants (raisins will do if you cannot find currants)

In a large mixing bowl, sift together the flour, yeast, sugar, and a teaspoon of salt. Then mix in the cinnamon, nutmeg, allspice, and dried currants into the flour. Make a small well in the middle of the dry ingredients and then pour in the milk, a quarter of a cup of warm water, the beaten egg, and the melted butter. Mix everything until it comes together in a large dough ball. If it seems to you that the dough is a bit too dry and not holding its shape, add a bit more water. On the other hand, if it feels too wet, give it a light dusting of flour.

Plop the dough onto a flour-dusted work surface and knead it with your hands until it feels smooth and a bit springy (press your thumb into the dough, if it rises back up then you are good). Transfer the dough into a greased bowl and cover using a clean, damp kitchen towel. Give it an hour or so to rise.

Once your dough has risen and doubled in size, plop it back onto a lightly-floured work surface. Knead the dough for a minute or so, and then divide the dough into roughly 12 even pieces. Shape each piece into a smooth ball and then transfer them onto a greased baking sheet. Take note that you should leave a bit of an allowance in between each bun to allow it to rise.

Using a small, very sharp knife, score a cross on the top of each bun and then cover the tray with a damp kitchen towel. Allow them to rise and double in size. While waiting for the buns to rise, preheat your oven to 220 degrees Celsius.

After letting the buns to rise and before placing the tray into the oven, mix some plain flour and water to create a thick paste. Pipe this flour paste into the crosses you cut into the top of the buns earlier. Allow the buns to bake for 15 to 20 minutes, or until they are golden brown and sound hollow when you tap on them. Mix a tablespoon of granulated sugar and some water and brush this mixture on the tops of buns right after you pull them out of the oven.

[21]

Earl Grey Teacakes

What goes better with tea other than teacakes that are actually infused with a refreshing tea flavor? Take note that this recipe will take quite a bit of time to make, so you better clear your schedule the morning before your afternoon tea because you will be quite busy making the Earl Grey Teacakes. But, you can be sure that the finished product will be worth every bit of your efforts.

Ingredients:

¾ of a cup of mixed dried fruits (you can choose any dried fruit mix you want)

The zest of half an orange

¾ of a cup of strong, hot, Earl Grey tea, made using two tea bags

1 cup of full cream milk

¾ of a stick of butter, frozen and cut into small cubes

2 cups of white bread flour

1 ½ teaspoon of allspice

¼ cup sugar

1 7g sachet of quick raising yeast

1 large organic egg, beaten lightly

Apricot jam for glazing

Place all of your dried fruits in a small bowl and pour the hot Earl Grey tea over them. Cover the bowl and steep the fruits in the tea overnight.

Pour the milk into a small saucepan and heat it until it is hot, but not scalding. Remove the saucepan from the heat and add the butter. Swirl the pan around to help melt the butter and cool the milk at the same time. Set it aside and allow it to cool.

In a large mixing bowl, combine the flour, sugar, yeast, allspice, and two pinches of salt. Make a well in the middle of the dry ingredients and pour in the cooled milk, the beaten egg, and a tablespoon of the tea you used to steep the fruits. Use a wooden spoon to combine all of the ingredients until it becomes doughy. Then tip the contents onto a lightly dusted board.

Knead the dough by hand for around 5 minutes or until the dough becomes springy. You can add a bit more flour if the dough seems too wet. After kneading, transfer the dough ball into a clean, greased bowl and cover it using a plastic cling wrap. Let the dough rise for around 2 hours or until it doubles in size.

After letting the dough rise, take off the cling wrap, knock out most of the air inside the dough and then add the tea-soaked fruits (strain any excess liquid if there is any). Knead the dough until all of the fruits are distributed evenly. If the fruits made the dough sticky then add a bit more flour.

Divide the dough into 6 balls and place them onto two, lightly dusted baking trays (3 per tray with plenty of space between them). Squash the dough balls lightly using your hands and then cover the trays loosely with some oiled plastic cling wrap and allow the dough to rise for a second time. While waiting for the dough to rise, preheat your oven to around 200 degrees Celsius.

Once the dough has risen, remove the plastic cover and plop the trays into the oven. Bake the teacakes for around 25 minutes, and swap the position of the trays halfway through to ensure even baking. Around 20 minutes into the baking time, take the teacakes out for a minute and brush their tops with some apricot jam, then place them back into the oven for another minute or so.

Let the teacakes cool down for a bit on a wire rack and serve them to your guests while they are still warm.

Biscuits and Cookies

Who does not like nibbling on a cookie while enjoying great tea and great company? Cookies and biscuits are relatively easy to make (compared to teacakes at least), and you can be sure to put a smile on your guests' faces when you serve them the kind of treats they enjoyed as a child.

Shortbread

Ingredients:

1 ½ cups of plain flour

2/3 of a cup of rice flour (you can find this in your local Asian foods store)

3 sticks of butter

2/3 cup of sugar, plus a bit more for topping the biscuits later

Using a food processor, combine the butter and sugar until smooth. Slowly add the other dry ingredients until everything is combined.

Spread the mixture on a lightly greased baking tray and cover the entire thing with plastic cling wrap. Make sure the surface is completely smooth. Place the baking tray in your fridge and let it set for at least 30 minutes (overnight is preferred). Preheat your oven to 180 degrees Celsius.

After the shortbread has spent enough time in the fridge, take it out and remove the plastic film. Poke holes all over the dough using a fork and sprinkle the rest of the sugar on top of it. Toss the baking tray into the oven and let it bake for around 20 to 25 minutes. Let it cool and then cut into bars and serve.

Chocolate Chunk Pecan Cookies

Ingredients:

1 200g bar of dark chocolate, cut into bite-size chunks

½ cup whole pecans

1 stick of butter

½ cup of flour

¼ cup of muscovado sugar

½ cup of brown sugar

A dash (or two) of vanilla extract

1 medium egg, lightly beaten

1 teaspoon baking soda

Preheat your oven to 180 degrees Celsius. Using a double boiler, melt 85 grams (roughly a third of a cup) of the dark chocolate. Then mix in the rest of the wet ingredients the flour, the baking soda and ¾ of the pecans, and the remaining chocolate.

Spoon the resulting mixture onto lightly oiled baking sheets (you could probably make around 12 cookies per tray). Press the remaining pecans and chocolate nuggets into the tops of the cookies.

Bake the cookies for around 12 to 15 minutes, or until the cookies are firm enough that they are able to hold their shape. Let the cookies cool on the tray before placing them on your serving dish.

The great thing about afternoon tea is that you can serve anything, as long as it is not too heavy. You can serve savory fares along with sweet ones; it is perfectly fine if you do. The recipes mentioned here are just some of the basic foods served during tea service. You can find many more recipe ideas online. You can even come up with your own; just let your imagination go wild.

Chapter 4 – Afternoon Tea Essentials

At this point, you already know what kinds of teas and pastries you need to serve for your afternoon tea party, but do you know how and where to serve your fares? In this chapter, you will learn the different components of a proper tea set and it may surprise you to know that you will need more than just simple teacups and saucers.

Choosing the Right Tea Set

Have you ever seen the Dowager Countess of Grantham drink her tea from a chipped mug from Disneyland? She will only drink tea from a proper teacup and only if it was served using a proper tea service.

The great thing about buying your own proper tea service is that you do not have to go about it piece by piece. You buy them as a complete set. The only problem you have now is figuring out which one of them you actually need.

How Many Guests Will You Have?

The first thing that you have to figure out before buying a tea set is how many people will you usually have over for afternoon tea? Are you only planning to have afternoon tea with your spouse or just one friend at a time? If so, then a 5-piece tea set (one teapot and two sets of teacups and saucers) may be all that you need. If you want to be a bit fancier, then you should purchase a matching creamer and sugar set too.

However, if you are planning to have several friends over for afternoon tea, then you will need one of the larger tea sets, like a 21-piece set for six people. These larger tea sets, besides the required teacups and teapots, also contain dessert dishes for serving the other food items on your afternoon tea menu.

How Large is Your Budget?

This should probably be higher up on this list since it does dictate the kind of tea set you can and cannot purchase. However, even if you have a somewhat limited budget, it is still possible for you to buy a nice tea set. It is not really a requirement for you to buy a brand new tea set. In fact, you really should try looking through flea markets and thrift shops for antique sets.

The great thing about tea sets is that their designs have hardly changed through the years. There are hardly any differences between a 20-year-old tea set and a brand new one, except perhaps for a bit of discoloration here and there.

Materials Used

Most of the tea sets available these days are made from glass, porcelain, ceramic, or silver. Each of these materials has its own pros and cons, and it would do you good to find out about them before you buy a set for yourself.

Glass – The great thing about glass tea sets is that they are beautiful and are relatively easy to match to any table setting. However, not many people recommend using glass tea sets because they are extremely fragile. For instance, if you pour tea that is too hot into a glass teapot or teacup, the sudden thermal shock could crack and shatter the glass.

Ceramic – Since you are planning to start hosting regular afternoon tea and since it is an English tradition, then you may not want to choose ceramic tea sets since these are usually used in Asian tea ceremonies. However, if you plan to mix up your usual afternoon tea occasionally and give it some oriental flavor, then you could get one set for your collection.

One thing to consider when buying ceramic tea sets, however, is that they are porous if they are unglazed. This means the taste of the tea will seep into the cups and teapots and will affect the taste of subsequent servings. To find out of the tea set you are buying is glazed or not, try running your fingers along the inside of the cups and teapots. If it is rough, then it is unglazed. If you do buy it, make sure that you will only use it for one particular type of tea.

Porcelain – One of the pros of using porcelain tea sets is that they have almost the same delicate look as that of glass sets, but they are more durable. The problem, however, is that porcelain, although most sets have really nice designs on them, can be difficult to match with other tableware. Although there are plain, monochrome porcelain tea sets, most of them do look a bit boring. The key to choosing a good porcelain tea set is to choose a neutral design that would go well with your other dining sets.

Silver – Tea sets made entirely of silver are probably the epitome of "fancy." Not only are these tea sets beautiful, they are also functional and very resistant to damage. On that note, silver tea sets do have a couple of notable drawbacks, the biggest of which is probably their price. Not only are you paying for the amount of craftsmanship that went into making silver tea sets, you are also paying for the precious metal they contain.

However, if you have some disposable income, you might want to invest in a good silver tea set because they do increase in value over time. Just make sure that you are getting actual silver pieces, not silver-plated ones.

Care and Maintenance

For all intents and purposes, it might be safe to assume that you will be choosing the porcelain tea sets for your first foray into the world of the English afternoon tea. In this part of the book, we will only concentrate on the care and maintenance of porcelain china sets.

Typically, porcelain tea sets are glazed inside and out. If your tea set falls under this category, then you can wash it the way you normally do. However, if it is unglazed, then you should just rinse the inside thoroughly using hot water and wipe away any loose tealeaves that are in there. Regardless of what the manufacturer says, you should not put your tea set in the dishwasher.

Another thing, even though porcelain and earthenware cups and pots can handle temperature changes better than glass, it does not mean that you can place the pots over a flame (unless it came with a specific tea warmer), or place the teapot and its contents in the freezer. Irresponsible use will still result to chipping and cracking so you should handle your tea set with care.

Flatware

The table setting for an afternoon tea service is not that different from that of other meals, albeit it contains fewer pieces of flatware. Keep in mind that you will be serving mostly finger foods so you do not have to go all out with your flatware setting. You will still need to provide forks (at the left side of the luncheon plates), a knife (to the right of the plate, blade facing inward), a butter knife (to the right of the knife, oriented the same way), a spoon (to the right of the knives), and a teaspoon (on the saucer besides the teacup).

As you can see, you may already have all the flatware needed for an afternoon tea service, especially if you are fond of having your friends and family over for dinner parties.

Chapter 5 – Proper Etiquette

Afternoon tea is not just about the food and drink. It is also about how you conduct yourself in the company of others. You may have noticed that whenever they have afternoon tea on *Downton Abbey*, even if the characters have some squabbles, they still refuse to forget their etiquette, which is as it should be.

Since only a handful of people have been groomed since childhood on the ways of proper etiquette and decorum regarding afternoon tea and high society, here are some do's and don'ts regarding afternoon tea.

Do not hook your finger into the handle of your teacup

When holding a teacup in your hand, place your fingers in the front and back of the handle, as if you are pinching it. You should never loop your finger inside the handle.

Do not raise your pinkie while drinking tea (or any kind of beverage for that matter)

This is one of the longest running afternoon tea faux pas ever. Some people say that raising the pinkie helps balance the cup while taking a sip, but this is not true. This practice is pointless and silly.

The proper way to stir your tea

Yes, there is a proper way to stir your tea. Say you have already poured cream and sugar into your teacup. The proper way to stir your tea is to start at six o'clock, and "cut" your tea towards the 12 o'clock position. Take extra care not to clink your teaspoon along the insides of your cup as it is considered improper. Also, remember that you should not leave your teaspoon inside the cup. After stirring your tea, remove your teaspoon and place it on the saucer provided.

Dress appropriately

Most venues that offer afternoon tea services do not really have a strict dress code, so you do not really have to require your guests to come in formal attire. However, that does not mean a shirt and jeans are acceptable. If you want to have a proper afternoon tea service, you and your guests should at least make an effort to dress up for the occasion. In most cases, a smart-casual look will work.

Do not dunk your biscuits or teacakes into your cup

This practice is only acceptable if you are doing it in the privacy of your own home without company. This type of behavior should never be displayed during an afternoon tea service. Take a bite of your scone and then take a sip of your tea. Do not attempt to do both things at once.

On the use of napkins

Fold your napkin in half and place it on your lap with the folded side facing you.

If you need to excuse yourself, do not place your napkin on the table. Place it on your seat and push the seat back into its proper place before you leave the room.

Do not use your napkin to wipe your face. Dab gently at the offending food particles until you have dislodged them.

Smoking is prohibited

Even if your afternoon tea is served outdoors on your patio, you still should not smoke. Besides the obvious negative health repercussions that smoking brings, the tobacco and smoke will also affect the way you taste the tea. Therefore, if you really want to enjoy every minute of your low tea service, then you should stifle your cravings for a cigarette, at least for an hour or two.

The proper way to drink tea

When drinking tea, sip and do not slurp. Tip the cup slightly towards your mouth and take small sips. You should also use tea to wash down your food. Swallow your food first before taking a sip of your tea.

If your tea is too hot, do not blow on it. Take small sips until your tea gets a bit cooler.

If you are not drinking your tea, place the cup onto the saucer. It is bad etiquette to talk extensively with your cup in your hands.

On eating scones

Traditional etiquette dictates that the proper way to eat scones is to break off small bite-sized pieces and then apply the desired amount of cream, butter, or jam before popping it into one's mouth. However, this rule has become lax and it is now socially acceptable to break the scone in half, top each half with your desired spread then take a bite.

Never use your teaspoon to apply the butter, jam, or cream to your scones

When scones are served with jam, butter, or cream, it always comes with a butter knife or spreader and you should use that instead.

Milk or tea first?

Surprisingly, this topic is still hotly debated. Some people are adamant that the milk should be poured into the teacups first before pouring in the tea. This practice actually started in the medieval days when cups were still made of "soft" paste porcelain.

People back then would pour milk into their cups first to temper the hot tea and prevent the cup from cracking. These days, however, porcelain cups are no longer as fragile as they used to be, so pouring tea before the milk is actually acceptable.

How to pour the tea

You should never fill your teacup to the brim. Always pour until the cup is around ¾ full to allow some room for sugar and/or milk. If your guests ask for "weak" tea, fill the cup halfway and then pour hot water up to the ¾ mark.

Even if you are hosting the afternoon tea in your own home, that does not mean the rules and etiquette no longer apply to you and your guests. If you truly want to have an authentic afternoon tea service, then you should do your best to follow the unwritten rules regarding it.

However, even though there are plenty of rules regarding etiquette during afternoon tea, it does not necessarily mean you should enforce them strictly. The whole point of having an afternoon tea service is to get together with the people you care about and catch up on each other's lives.

If you have to point out each and every mistake your guests make, then it does not make you a gracious host. If you want your guests to follow the unwritten etiquette governing the afternoon tea service, practice it yourself and they will most likely follow suit.

***

Receive e-mail updates on new book releases and free book promotions from Tadio Diller. By visiting the link below

http://bit.ly/list_tadiodiller_cs

***

Conclusion

Thank you again for buying this book!

I hope this book was able to help you understand the practice of the afternoon tea service much better. Thanks to shows like *Downton Abbey*, people are now getting more interested in the fancy way of living, which is always a good thing because people could always stand to have a little more culture in their lives.

The next step is to start hunting for all of the things you will need for your very first tea service. Consult this book as often as you need to make sure that your initial foray into the fancy world of tea culture will go as smoothly as possible.

Finally, if you enjoyed this book, then I'd like to ask you for a favor. Would you be kind enough to leave a review for this book on Amazon? It'd be greatly appreciated!

Thank you and good luck!

***

Receive e-mail updates on new book releases and free book promotions from Tadio Diller. By visiting the link below

http://bit.ly/list_tadiodiller_cs

***

Check Out My Other Books!

You will find these books by simply searching for them on Amazon.com

For too many people wine can be a little intimidating. You may know you love the taste of a red or a white wine, but how do you know what kind of wine to order at a restaurant? How can you choose the right wine for your dinner party when there are so many options?

If you've wondered why whiskey is so popular or what the real difference is between scotch and bourbon this book is for you. Packed with interesting facts and whiskey cocktail recipes, this book tells you all you ever wanted to know about whiskey. This book explains what proof is and why it matters so much for your whiskey.

Tea is the most popular drink in the world. Not even the biggest soda companies in the world can match the number of dedicated drinkers tea boasts. From China to England, tea is seen as a delicious and relaxing drink.

The book shows you how to make sure your next party is unforgettable. With the tips and recipes in this book you will be able to make all of your favorite cocktails right in your own home.

A single cup of delicious, life affirming coffee can set you back two bucks or more at your local coffee shop. Did you know you can make coffee at home that not only costs much less, but actually tastes even better than what you are getting at the coffee shop?

This book will show you everything you ever wanted to know about beer from its history to how to find the perfect beer for any meal. It will introduce you to new beers and help you explore beers beyond the common big commercial light beers.

Greetings from the Lean Stone Publishing Company

We want to thank you so much for reading this book to the end. We are committed to creating life changing books in the Self Help area, such as this one that you just read.

If you liked this book and want to follow us for more information on upcoming book launches, free promotions and special offers, then follow us on Facebook and Twitter!

Sign up for e-mail updates on new releases and free promotions by visiting this link:

http://bit.ly/list_lsp_cs

Like us: **www.facebook.com/leanstonepublishing**

Follow: **@leanstonebooks**

Thank you again for reading to the end, it means the world to us!

Made in the
USA
Middletown, DE